Chapter 1

Introduction

And the test of all of us—for all of us had our origins on the other side of the sea—is whether we will assist in enabling America to live her separate and independent life, retaining our ancient affections, indeed, but determining everything we do by the interests that exist on this side of the sea.

—Woodrow Wilson

As the United States continues to struggle with charting a coherent foreign policy course in today's post-Cold War world, it finds itself confronted by an international landscape far less clearly defined than that of the past fifty years. The overwhelming clarity of purpose provided by the Soviet threat has been swept away. In its place we find the dynamics of an increasingly interdependent global economy being played out against the backdrop of emerging regional tensions precipitated by long-dormant causes and hatreds finding new voice after years of repression. At the same time, we find an increasing roster of domestic players in the foreign policy arena who, as Donald Snow and Eugene Brown point out, no longer subscribe to the theory that "politics ends at the water's edge."[1] In this turbulent arena where foreign policy and domestic political issues converge, we see the emergence of America's ethnic minorities as a potentially significant force in the equation. In examining exactly what role these oft-overlooked foreign policy players occupy, this paper focuses first on a discussion of the growing political clout ethnic groups wield in this country. From there it examines two post-

World War II cases where ethnic groups within the United States have successfully influenced foreign policy: 1) Jewish-Americans and our policies toward Israel, and 2) Irish-Americans and our policies toward Northern Ireland. To provide some contrast to these successful groups the paper then examines two groups who initially met with failure in their efforts to influence foreign policy: 1) Armenian-Americans and the Armenian Question, and 2) Arab-Americans and U.S. Middle East Policy. For both groups the paper also explores their efforts to learn from the experiences of others and some more recent limited successes based upon that experience. Finally, the paper discusses the impact these emerging political influences may have on foreign policy priorities and their implications for the future.

Notes

[1] Donald M. Snow and Eugene Brown, *Beyond the Water's Edge: An Introduction to U.S. Foreign Policy* (New York: St. Martin's Press, 1997), 1.

Chapter 2

The Growing Political Power of America's Ethnic Groups

The political influence of ethnic groups in the United States is not a recent phenomenon. In major cities such as New York, Boston, and Chicago the impact at the local level has been a prominent feature of the political landscape since the great influx of European immigrants in the late 1800's and early 1900's. The wise politician in those local arenas was quick to appeal to ethnic pride in his dealings with the locals:

> Thus, New York's most celebrated mayor, Jimmy "the Hat" Walker, would often begin a speech with numerous "city comparisons." New York, he would tell his audience, had more Irish than Dublin, more Jews then Jerusalem, more Italians than Rome, and so on, his examples confined only by his geographical recollection on that day.[1]

The ethnic vote has also played an increasingly important role in politics at the national level, due in large part to two critical factors. The first is simply a matter of numbers: the 1990 Census showed that foreign-born persons numbered 20 million and comprised eight percent of the total population.[2] The trends indicate Hispanics will replace blacks as the dominant minority by 2010.[3] In addition, projections are that the white majority, just over 75 percent in 1990, will continue to fall and approach a "majority minority" by 2050.[4]

The second significant factor as it relates to ethnic political potential at the national level is the tendency for these groups to concentrate in the large cities of states with a significant number of electoral votes.[5] The six states of California (54 electoral votes in

1996), New York (33), Florida (25), Texas (32), New Jersey (15), and Illinois (22) accounted for 73 percent of the 20 million foreign-born persons included in the 1990 Census.[6] While the electoral votes cited were based on estimated data from the 1990 Census[7], the message is clear:

> When victory margins in these states start shrinking below 4 percentage points (as they do in all but aberrant elections), it behooves the candidates to take a good long look at the votes of ethnics and the manner in which they can be influenced.[8]

Compounding the potential effects of this influence within the Electoral College framework is the tendency for particular ethnic communities to vote in blocs. When Mexican-Americans turned out in support of the Kennedy-Johnson ticket in 1960, they did so in record numbers and awarded 85 percent of their vote to the ticket. Likewise in 1964, Johnson captured a significant majority of Mexican- and Jewish-American vote.[9] This phenomenon is not surprising given that political parties within the U.S. consistently target ethnic groups for votes and contributions. In a July 1997 article discussing the impact of ethnic groups on foreign policy, *U.S. News and World Report* indicated that the Democratic National Committee had specifically targeted not only Asian-Americans during the last campaign, but also Poles, Greeks, Irish, Lithuanians, Hungarians, Croatians, and Albanians.[10]

The potential political power of ethnic groups does not in and of itself translate into an ability to influence foreign policy decisions. Sheer numbers do not necessarily generate political power unless the group can somehow be motivated to exert that power through the physical act of voting. What this discussion does suggest is that ethnic groups exist now with sufficient numbers to be a force on the political scene, and if sufficiently motivated, can exert an influence which representatives at all levels ignore at their political peril. The discussion in the following chapter centers on two cases where

the requisite motivation existed and the Jewish- and Irish-American communities were

successful at influencing foreign policy decisions.

Notes

[1] Mark R. Levy and Michael S. Kramer, *The Ethnic Factor* (New York: Simon and Schuster, 1972), 10.

[2] Barry R. Chiswick and Teresa A. Sullivan, "The New Immigrants," in *State of the Union: America in the 1990s, Volume Two: Social Trends*, ed. Reynolds Farley (New York: Russell Sage Foundation, 1995), 212.

[3] Roderick J. Harrison and Claudette E. Bennett, "Racial and Ethnic Diversity," in *State of the Union: America in the 1990s, Volume Two: Social Trends* (New York: Russell Sage Foundation, 1995), 149.

[4] Ibid., 141.

[5] Levy and Kramer, *The Ethnic Factor*, 208-209.

[6] Chiswick and Sullivan, "The New Immigrants," 227.

[7] David W. Abbott and James P. Levine, *Wrong Winner: The Coming Debacle in the Electoral College* (New York: Praeger Publishers, 1991), 6-8.

[8] Levy and Kramer, 209.

[9] Ibid., 16-17.

[10] Paul Glastris, "Multicultural Foreign Policy in Washington," *U.S. News and World Report,* 21 July 1997, 34.

Chapter 3

Breaking the Code: Successful Group Pressure

In searching for examples of the effective marshalling of ethnic group pressure with respect to foreign policy decisions, one is hard pressed to identify two more successful groups than Jewish- and Irish-Americans.

The Jewish-American Lobby and U.S. Policy toward Israel

The United States has played a significant role in the affairs of the State of Israel since its inception and throughout that time the Jewish-American community has played an important part in ensuring foreign policy decisions were on the whole supportive. It is not the intent of this paper to outline these interactions in detail, but simply to provide an overview of the process. The available literature indicates that pressure from the Jewish community was present as discussions on the establishment of a Jewish state in Palestine were coming to a head in 1947. Various competing proposals were circulating with regard to Partition or Trusteeship, and the idea of a separate Jewish state found little favor within the State Department. Their position centered around the argument that Britain had been able to maintain reasonably good relations within the region by dealing with the Arab states. If the United States was now to assume the mantle of Western leadership in the region, the State Department's position was that this Arab-centered policy was the correct one to follow. Inherent in their argument was a belief that if the Arabs felt alienated by the West through the establishment of a Jewish state in their midst, they would turn to the Soviet Union, which would welcome the opportunity to gain a foothold in the region.[1]

Despite these compelling arguments from State against supporting the Jewish cause, arguments President Truman would heed elsewhere in the world where potential Communist gains were involved, the decision was made to recognize the State of Israel in 1948 when the Jewish minority in Palestine declared their independence. While theories put forward to explain this decision are often couched in terms of concern for humanitarian issues and guilt in the aftermath of the Holocaust, the underlying motivation seems to have been political.[2] Indeed, in 1946 when Truman first announced his support for the concept of a Jewish state, his advisors were advocating such a step to help bolster sagging Democratic prospects in the upcoming New York congressional elections.[3] As Truman himself would explain to members of the State Department voicing concerns about his direction on the issue, "I am sorry, gentlemen, but I have to answer to hundreds of thousands who are anxious for the success of Zionism: I do not have hundreds of thousands of Arabs among my constituents."[4]

Since this early success in influencing U.S. foreign policy, Jewish-Americans have become far more sophisticated in their approach to the issue of support for Israel. The power of politics still remains the bedrock of their group power. Although relatively small in numbers compared to other ethnic groups, Jewish-Americans consistently lead the way in terms of voter turnout. As with ethnic groups as a whole, they are congregated in key electoral vote states. Unlike many of the other groups, however, the Jewish community is also able to impact elections by making significant campaign contributions.[5]   In addition to the block vote power wielded by Jewish-Americans, several official domestic lobbying groups have been formed to focus attention on the Israeli position.   The American Israel Public Affairs Committee (AIPAC) attempts to influence legislation by providing information to members of Congress on issues that affect Israeli interests.   Their arguments carefully stress why any position they advocate is in keeping with U.S. national interests.   This tactic helps to avoid some of the criticism their activities have generated in the past.   Another influential group is the Conference of Presidents of Major American Jewish Organizations, which represents the membership of thirty-eight separate groups and serves to provide a united front for their position on foreign policy matters.   While AIPAC targets the legislative branch of government, the Conference of Presidents serves as the conduit to the executive branch.[6]   Implicit in any dealings with these groups by members of Congress and even the President, is the ability to support their friends by delivering political and financial rewards.

The Jewish-American community's efforts to influence American foreign policy towards Israel have for the most part been successful.   While there have been partial defeats along the way, such as the sale of AWACS aircraft to Saudi Arabia during the Reagan Administration, there is no question that the group exerts significant influence over the process of developing foreign policy toward Israel.   According to Mitchell Bard, the success stems from the advantages the group enjoys "in every area considered relevant to interest group influence.   It has

> a) a large and vocal membership; b) members who enjoy high status and legitimacy; c) a high degree of electoral participation (voting and financing); d) effective leadership; e) a high degree of access to decision-makers; and f) public support.   More over, for reasons at least partly attributable to the lobby's efforts, the lobby's primary objective—a U.S. commitment to Israel—has been accepted as *a* national interest.[7]

8

To much the same extent, the same analysis can be applied to our next ethnic group case—the Irish-Americans.

Irish-Americans and U.S. Policy toward Northern Ireland

Irish-Americans, perhaps due to the circumstances under which many of their ancestors departed Ireland, have always maintained a special affinity for the homeland they left behind. In the early days of Irish immigration, this manifested itself in unquestioned support for the cause of Irish nationalism. Indeed, between 1848 and 1900, Irish-Americans contributed $260 million to Ireland and prompted historian Lawrence McCaffrey to remark, "From the time of the Great Famine in the mid-1840s until the conclusion of the Anglo-Irish War (1921), Irish-American fanaticism and money sustained Irish Nationalism."[8] By the mid-1900s, however, this rabid nationalism had waned, in large part due to the "suburbanization" of large numbers of Irish-Americans who found their new middle-class lifestyles less accommodating of violent political associations. While the volatile climate of the late-1960s, when political protests in this country coincided with civil rights protests by the Catholic minority in Northern Ireland, partially awakened this dormant national feeling, it would never again gain the sense of urgency of earlier times. Financial support for the Irish Northern Aid Committee, popularly known as NORAID, was initially strong but subsided as questions arose concerning how the money was being spent at the Irish end. Even so, while never reaching the level of support shown earlier in the century, contributions to the organization served as a lifeline for the families of jailed IRA members and, more controversially, served other IRA requirements.[9]

On the political front, significant events were portended by Jimmy Carter's 1976 campaign platform, which included a call for the eventual reunification of Ireland. Whether this was a legitimate manifestation of Carter's preoccupation with human rights issues or, as was believed by British observers, "a political imperative for practically every major U.S. politician, especially Democrats, to at least mouth such sentiments" is open to debate. This belief was based in the realization that while the Irish-American community does not bloc vote as consistently as Jewish-Americans, their political clout is still significant and makes outright support of British policies in Northern Ireland unwise.[10]

Policy toward Ireland at the time was essentially the domain of four enormously influential Irish-American politicians, known as the "Four Horsemen:" former New York Governor Hugh Carey, Senator Daniel Patrick Moynihan, Speaker of the House Tip O'Neill, and Senator Edward Kennedy. Feeling the climate was right for a major policy statement on the situation in Northern Ireland, they urged President Carter to pledge U.S. government aid and corporate investment. The resulting presidential statement, issued in August 1977, made the aid contingent upon an end to the violence and acceptance of a political settlement.[11]

At the same time the "Four Horsemen" were pursuing a fairly limited agenda through the President, Congressman Mario Biaggi was in the process of forming an Ad Hoc Committee on Irish Affairs. Despite having no legislative authority, the committee generated enough political capital through its attacks on the excesses of police interrogation techniques in Northern Ireland and other issues to entice almost a third of the House of Representatives' 435 members to sign up.[12]

Despite these tentative steps, it would be another nine years before the United States would become directly involved in any substantive way with a meaningful settlement proposal involving the British government and the Irish. Financial support for the Anglo-Irish Agreement in 1986 helped underscore the significance of this step on the road to a final settlement, albeit a partial one in which the British recognized the Irish Republic's role in the Northern Ireland debate. The U.S., for its part, now has a vested interest in seeing the process continue toward an ultimate solution.[13]

Despite the fact that these recent U.S. foreign policy moves concerning Northern Ireland were influenced by prominent Irish-American politicians, the catalyst for their actions was the very real desire of the Irish-American population to see an end to the conflict. While the fervent nationalism of the past is fading, it refuses to die completely.

> Yet the American connection remains. It is linked to Ireland by more than utopian aspirations of revolutionary gunrunners. Among Irish-Americans it is sustained as much, if not more, by feelings for the past as it is by hopes for the future. For America's relationship with Ireland is a complex, Janus-like one, in which the past and future mingle and often cannot be distinguished from each other, in which the politician has a role along with the rebel.[14]

Notes

[1] Cheryl A. Rubenberg, *Israel and the American National Interest: A Critical Examination* (Urbana, Ill.: University of Illinois Press, 1986), 32.

[2] Ibid., 8.

[3] Ibid., 32.

[4] Ibid., 31.

[5] Mitchell Geoffrey Bard, *The Water's Edge and Beyond: Defining the Limits to Domestic Influence on United States Middle East Policy* (New Brunswick, N.J.: Transaction Publishers, 1991), 7-8.

[6] Ibid., 12-13.

[7] Ibid., 18.

[8] Jack Holland, *The American Connection: U.S. Guns, Money, and Influence in Northern Ireland* (New York: Viking Press, 1987), 26.

[9] Ibid., 31.

Notes

[10] Kevin J. Kelley, *The Longest War: Northern Ireland and the IRA* (Westport, Conn.: Lawrence Hill and Company, Inc., 1988), 277.

[11] Ibid., 277-278.

[12] Ibid., 280.

[13] Holland, *The American Connection*, 151.

[14] Ibid., 6.

Chapter 4

Unsuccessful Group Influence and the Learning Curve

While Jewish and Irish-Americans have proven themselves relatively successful at securing support for their causes within the American political system, others have not fared as well. The experiences of Armenian- and Arab-Americans serve as a useful counterpoint to the previous discussion. While both groups have historically had to deal with failure in championing their respective causes with respect to U.S. foreign policy, the research shows a movement along the learning curve that has produced more recent successes or at least a more encouraging trend.

Armenian-Americans and U.S. Policy toward the Armenian Question

While the history of ethnic Armenians as a definable group within American society really began in the late nineteenth century, their arrival on these shores was simply the latest manifestation of a diaspora that had its roots nearly seven centuries earlier. To understand the motivations of Armenian-Americans with respect to their homeland, it is essential to have a basic knowledge of the events that shaped their collective history.

The Armenian people can trace their heritage in the region of present-day Armenia and Western Turkey back to at least 550 B.C. when they were first mentioned in Greek writings of the times.[1] The Armenian state was the first to adopt Christianity as its official religion in A.D. 301, an identification proudly proclaimed throughout its history and one at least partially to blame for the level of persecution suffered during later generations.[2] In addition to a religious affiliation which made them distinct from the majority of peoples in the region, the Armenians suffered from a geo-strategic location which placed them squarely in the path of every marauding conqueror to arrive on the scene from Asia, the Middle East, or Russia. Beginning in the eleventh century, the invasions of the Seljuq Turks, the Mongols, Tamerlane, and the Ottoman Turks scattered the Armenian population throughout the Middle East, Western Europe, and Russia.

> For Armenians these centuries were truly a "dark age," one in which the settled agricultural population of Eastern Anatolia suffered from the inroads of the nomads and the destructive fighting between the Turks and the Persians. As a result, large numbers left their homeland for life in exile, and the Armenians, like the Jews, became a stateless people.[3]

Like the Jewish people, shared religion and culture proved strong bonds for the Armenians. By the late nineteenth century, the nationalistic tide sweeping through Europe had also infected the Armenian community. This movement coincided with the decline of the Ottoman Empire and the advance of Russia into the region. As the Russians continued to press the Ottomans in the Caucasus, the average Armenian peasant living in the eastern provinces of the Empire began to look favorably on the prospect of eventually falling under Russian rule. In fact, large numbers of them had already migrated toward Transcaucasia (roughly the combined area of Georgia, Armenia, and Azerbaijan today) following its annexation by the Russian Empire early in the century.[4] These attitudes, coupled with active participation by Caucasian Armenians on the Russian side during the Russo-Turkish War of 1877-1878 and the actions of Armenian nationalists within the Ottoman Empire in the early 1890s sparked a brutal response from the Turks. During the period 1894-1896 the Ottoman Empire massacred 300,000 Armenians[5], prompting an increase in the diaspora's population and the first sizable wave of migration to the United States. In 1894 50,000 Armenians arrived on U.S. soil and by 1899 their numbers would swell to 70,000.[6] The new immigrants brought with them the memories of their long struggle for a national homeland and the vivid recollections of their persecution at the hands of the Ottoman Empire.

At the same time, the struggle continued back in Transcaucasia with the Dashnak party "calling on all Armenians—including the young, the old, the rich, the women, the priests—to support the "people's war" and the "Sacred Task" against the Turkish government."[7] The Armenians remaining within the Ottoman Empire consequently bore the brunt of retaliations for the actions of the Nationalists. With the outbreak of World War I, the Ottoman Turks saw an opportunity to resolve the Armenian problem once and for all. While specifics are debated between the opposing sides, what seems clear is that through a combination of forced relocation, starvation, and outright massacre, the Ottoman Turks brutally disposed of nearly 1.5 million Armenians in 1915-1916.[8] Described by U.S. Ambassador Henry Morgenthau as "the murder of a nation," the Armenian Genocide sparked outrage throughout the world. Relief efforts were generated within the U.S. by the Armenian Relief Committee, which raised $100,000 in the first month and $11,000,000 by the war's end.[9]

The outbreak of revolution in Russia during October 1917 led to the withdrawal of troops from the Caucasus and created a window of opportunity for Armenian nationalists to form an independent Armenian republic in May 1918. Armenian forces continued to fight for the Allied cause in the region until the surrender of the Ottomans in October.[10] In the Resolution of the Five Powers, signed in January of 1919 by the United States among others, the following pledge was made:

> ...because of the historic misgovernment of the Turks of subject peoples and the terrible massacres of Armenians and others in recent years, the Allied and Associated Powers are agreed that Armenia, Syria, Mesopotamia, Palestine, and Arabia must be completely severed from the Turkish Empire.[11]

The United States, however, had never declared war on the Ottoman Empire and so was in no position to dictate the terms of a final settlement. The original agreement, approved by the Allies at the San Remo conference in 1920, provided for an Armenian republic whose disputed borders with Turkey would be determined by President Woodrow Wilson. Known as the Treaty of Sèvres, the agreement was signed by representatives of the Ottoman Empire in August despite dictating a significant loss of territory and the internationalization of the Straits.[12]

The seizure of power by the Turkish Nationalists under Kemal Atatürk spelled the end of the Ottoman Empire. As a result, the new Turkish government felt no obligation to abide by the Treaty of Sèvres and moved to consolidate its territorial boundaries. They immediately regained eastern Anatolia, and by March 1921 had signed a treaty with the Russians delineating the boundaries between the two countries. This denied the Armenians any possibility of reestablishing their traditional homeland. The event also witnessed the first attempts by the fledgling Armenian-American interest groups to influence foreign policy by calling for a rejection of the Lausanne Treaty which had been drafted to replace the stillborn Sèvres Treaty. In particular the American Committee Opposed to the Lausanne Treaty, dominated by an Armenian-American named Vahan Cardashian, lobbied the Senate to reject the treaty.[13] Treaty opponents had an ally in the Senate as William King of Utah summed up the arguments against, focusing specifically upon what many felt were broken promises to the Armenian people, whose plight was totally ignored in the Lausanne document. In the end, the failure of the treaty to fulfill

American promises was a major cause for its defeat. While the Armenian-Americans could be considered successful in their fight against the Lausanne Treaty, the final outcome was still a failure for the Armenian cause. Their homeland was now split between the Turkish and Soviet states and the U.S. government essentially abandoned any further support for the Armenian position when they exchanged diplomatic notes with the Turks and proceeded on with normalized relations without a formal treaty in-place.[14]

Contemporary efforts by Armenian-American groups to influence foreign policy have, however, been more successful. Part of this is attributable to an increase in overall numbers and part to a rise in the level of sophistication of their efforts. There are nearly one million Armenian-Americans, today located primarily in the key electoral states of New Jersey, New York, California, and Illinois.[15] The Armenian community's concerns are represented by several national organizations: the Armenian Assembly, the Armenian National Committee of America (ANCA), and the Armenian American Action Committee.[16]

Starting in 1988 when an earthquake leveled much of the country, Armenian-American organizations funneled money and relief supplies to the area. Following the demise of the Soviet Union, Armenian-Americans have provided the political clout to ensure Armenia receives the second highest level of U.S. aid to the Newly Independent States and the highest per capita aid.[17] The Armenian lobby also managed to have a provision inserted into the 1992 Freedom Support Act (Section 907) which restricts U.S. aid to Azerbaijan until that country abandons its blockade of Armenia and the Nagorno-Karabakh region.[18] This past year Armenian-Americans raised $11 million through a telethon in Los Angeles to finance improvements to the road transportation infrastructure between Armenia and Nagorno-Karabakh.[19] Finally, Armenian groups in this country continue to press for official recognition of the Armenian Genocide to include a day to honor those who were killed. This is an extremely sensitive subject with the Turks, who have never formally recognized their role in the atrocity.[20]

The Armenian-Americans represent an ethnic group that showed little early success in forging foreign policy agendas. Their perseverance and willingness to apply the tactics employed successfully by other groups have paid dividends recently.

Arab-Americans and Middle East Policy

Another group which has had a marked lack of success in the foreign policy arena is the Arab-Americans. Perhaps the most compelling reason for this lack of success is that the group finds itself face-to-face with the powerful Jewish-American lobby on most issues. Just as their brethren in the Middle East have found themselves consistently on the losing side in their military conflicts with the State of Israel over the course of the years, so too the Arab-American lobby has found itself outmaneuvered at almost every turn by the Jewish-Americans. There are several reasons for this historically poor track record, not the least of which is the diversity of opinions within the Arab community on issues affecting the Middle East. Whereas it is relatively easy for the various Jewish organizations to keep tuned in to the latest position of the Jewish State, it is exceedingly difficult to keep one's finger on the pulse of what the latest thoughts are from Egypt, Syria, Jordan, etc. This leaves the Arab-American groups without a coherent "party line" to argue for.[21]

A second reason for their lack of success is the fact that just as the various nations that make up the Arab world have a diverse range of opinions on issues, so too do the members of the Arab-American community. They are divided by these diverse origins and have traditionally not been politically motivated. While they do form organizations, these usually tend to be social, cultural, educational, or charitable.[22] There are some 400 local Arab-American groups spread throughout the country. These usually have limited memberships and are run on tight budgets by one-man deep administrative staffs. Historically it has also not helped the cause to have many of these organizations, whether in their speeches or their publications, take a fairly radical tone which often alienates the American audience at-large from the start.[23]

Another significant hindrance to the effectiveness of Arab-Americans in influencing foreign policy is that their approach has been reactive rather than proactive. In most cases the Arab lobby reacts to what Israel is doing or has done. The message, therefore, is anti-Israel rather than pro-Arab. This approach, necessitated to a certain extent by a lack of consensual policy positions amongst the community, sets an overall negative tone and does not allow for a well-orchestrated campaign.[24]

If one looks back through the discussion of the Jewish-American lobby, for each success mentioned there in influencing U.S. foreign policy a corresponding failure can be added to the Arab-American tally. Just like the Armenians, however, the Arab-Americans are steadily climbing the learning curve. Arabs are organizing into larger organizations which should produce greater leverage in their confrontations with the Jewish lobby. The Action Committee on American Arab Relations (ACAAR) is one, as is the National Association of Arab-Americans. They have also learned the power of a positive message and find themselves more successful discussing issues in terms of, for example, pro-Palestinian consequences. If they continue to apply the lessons learned during their long confrontation with the Jewish lobby, they should find themselves continuing to improve their success rate.

Notes

[1] Dennis R. Papazian, "Armenians," *The Armenian Genocide* homepage, page 1 of 11; on-line, Internet, 13 January 1999, available from http://www.calpoly.edu/~pkiziria /pub-files/history.html.

[2] Ibid., 3.

[3] Ronald Grigor Suny, ed., *Transcaucasia, Nationalism, and Social Change: Essays in the History of Armenia, Azerbaijan, and Georgia* (Ann Arbor, Mich.: The University of Michigan Press, 1996), 4-5.

[4] Ibid., 146.

[5] Ibid., 160.

[6] Kathleen Newland, "The Impact of U.S. Refugee Policies on U.S. Foreign Policy: A Case of the Tail Wagging the Dog?," in *Threatened Peoples, Threatened Borders: World Migration and U.S. Policy,* eds. Michael S. Teitelbaum and Myron Weiner (New York: The American Assembly, 1995), page 10 of 13; on-line, Internet, 15 January 1999, available from http://www.ceip.org/people/migdog.htm.

[7] Suny, *Transcaucasia, Nationalism, and Social Change,* 151.

[8] Papazian, "Armenians," 10.

[9] Roger R. Trask, *The United States Response to Turkish Nationalism and Reform, 1914-1939* (Minneapolis, Minn.: The University of Minnesota Press, 1971), 20-21.

[10] "Armenia," *Library of Congress Country Study,* n.p.; on-line, Internet, 15 January 1999, available from http://rs6.loc.gov/cgi-bin/query/r?frd/cstdy:@field(DOCID+am0020

[11] *The Lausanne Treaty: Turkey and Armenia* (New York: The American Committee Opposed to the Lausanne Treaty, 1926), 14.

[12] Trask, 27.

[13] Ibid., 38.

[14] Ibid., 51.

[15] F. Wallace Hays, "U.S. Congress and the Caspian," *Caspian Crossroads* 3, no. 3 (Winter 1998): 8.

[16] Newland, "The Impact of U.S. Refugee Policies," 10.

[17] Ibid., 10.

[18] Ibid., 10.

[19] *News from Armenia and Artsakh/Karabagh,* page 3 of 4; on-line, Internet, 15 January 1999, available from http://www.erols.com/guerig/v1/armenia.html.

[20] Newland, 10.

Notes

[21] Robert H. Trice, "Domestic Interest Groups and the Arab-Israeli Conflict: A Behavioral Analysis," in *Ethnicity and U.S. Foreign Policy,* ed. Abdul Aziz Said (New York: Praeger Publishers, 1977), 135.

[22] Steven L. Spiegel, "Ethnic Politics and the Formulation of U.S. Policy Toward the Arab-Israeli Dispute," in *Ethnic Groups and U.S. Foreign Policy,* ed. Mohammed E. Ahari (New York: Greenwood Press, 1987), 26.

[23] Trice, "Domestic Interest Groups and the Arab-Israeli Conflict," 121.

[24] Spiegel, "Ethnic Politics and the Formulation of U.S. Policy," 28.

Chapter 5

Implications for Future Foreign Policy Priorities

To this point we have seen how the rapidly growing ethnic population within the United States represents significant potential political power and, through the examples of the Jewish- and Irish-American communities, have seen how this political influence can have an impact on foreign policy decisions. We have also witnessed how other groups have been equally unsuccessful, but have learned from their mistakes. What conclusions can be drawn with regard to their potential impact on future foreign policy decisions?

As mentioned earlier, the post-Cold War world is drastically changed from the paradigm we grew accustomed to during the past fifty years. Strong historical pressures for self-determination, often fueled by intense nationalism or ethnic hatred, have outlived the political system that kept them in check for so many years. We see these pressures reemerging at a time when the threat to our national existence posed by the Soviet Union has essentially disappeared and no legitimate threat of equal magnitude is on the horizon.

One aspect of the census data that was not discussed earlier was the diversity of ethnic origin reflected in the census data. The 1990 Census listed more than 250 areas claimed as place of origin by the respondents. This did not include categories reflecting the breakup of the Soviet Union, Czechoslovakia, and Yugoslavia, a fact which will significantly expand the list in the next census.[1] One implication of these numbers is that the more ethnic groups you have represented in the population, the greater the chances that some of them will have arrived in this country steeped in nationalist traditions that seek self-determination for their ancestral homeland. Like the Irish-Americans, these dreams can be sustained for long periods of time on hope and merely await the opportunity, through the political process in their new home, to apply pressure through foreign policy channels to effect an outcome favorable to their cause. At the same time, the technological revolution provides these recent immigrants with more accessible communications with those he or she left behind. In addition to keeping the new immigrant instantaneously updated on what is happening on the political front "back home," this link reduces the individual's need to adjust to the new environment. As Abdul Aziz Said contends in *Ethnicity and U.S. Foreign Policy,* "Mass communication, instead of unifying mankind, is paradoxically differentiating him into progressively smaller communities."[2]

Another implication to be gleaned from both cases is that an ethnic group has a better chance of effectively influencing foreign policy if their cause can be seen to be in keeping with the national interests of the United States. While some may argue as to whether the establishment of the State of Israel back in 1948 was truly in keeping with our national interests at the time, within ten years the fact that Israel was serving as a counter-balance for growing Soviet influence in the region was a significant factor in our Middle East strategy. The task of proving this connection may, in fact, be somewhat simplified today with the lack of a clear threat and clearly defined national interests.

James Schlesinger contends that U.S. foreign policy today is a result of "the stapling together of a series of goals put forth by domestic constituency groups."[3]

One national interest that has remained reasonably well articulated in the National Security Strategy is the fostering of democratic forms of government throughout the world. An ethnic group with the ability to energize its members for the cause at least has an opportunity to influence American policymakers, even though outright military aid is not likely. The Jewish community is a perfect example, albeit one endowed with far more advantages than the majority of ethnic groups will be able to muster.

While we have focused primarily on efforts by ethnic groups to influence foreign policy toward a positive outcome for their own agenda, the same issues relate to exerting influence to deny an adversary a positive outcome. The trick is in packaging the proposals and again the key is couching the debate in terms of U.S. national interests. If your group's position is perceived to be more closely aligned with these interests, you win. If not, you lose. It is also important to recognize that your audience in this debate is not the entire American population. The focus of an interest group's efforts is the decision-maker possessing the power to influence events. Jürgen Habermas described the differences in public and quasi-public opinion in the following manner:

> These formal opinions [quasi-public opinion] can be traced back to specific institutions: they are officially or semi-officially authorized as announcements, proclamations, declarations, and speeches. Here we are dealing with opinions that circulate in a relatively narrow circle—skipping the mass of the population—between the large political press and, generally, those publicist organs that cultivate rational debate and the advising, influencing, and deciding bodies with political or politically relevant jurisdictions (cabinet, government commissions, administrative bodies, parliamentary committees, corporate bureaucracies, and union secretariats).[4]

Provided the case is made coherently to the decision maker and the recommended action is in keeping with the fairly broad categories of national interest, the fairly narrow interests of a particular group may well prevail.

Notes

[1] Barry R. Chiswick and Teresa A. Sullivan, "The New Immigrants," in *State of the Union: America in the 1990s, Volume Two: Social Trends,* ed. Reynolds Farley (New York: Russell Sage Foundation, 1995), 225.

[2] Abdul Aziz Said, "A Redefinition of National Interest, Ethnic Consciousness, and U.S. Foreign Policy," in *Ethnicity and U.S. Foreign Policy,* ed. Abdul Aziz Said (New York: Praeger Publishers, 1977), 4.

[3] Quoted in Samuel P. Huntington, "The Erosion of American National Interests," *Foreign Affairs,* 76, no. 5 (September/October 1997): 40.

[4] Jürgen Habermas, "On the Concept of Public Opinion," in *The Habermas Reader,* ed. William Outhwaite (Oxford, U.K.: Blackwell Publishers Ltd, 1996), 37.

Chapter 6

Conclusion

> Will a group's views of America's national interest be neglected because
> of the group's size, skin color, religion, or country of origin? Can anyone
> be excluded from the formation of a true national interest? It is the ethnic
> interest groups, because of their ties, passions, and preoccupations that
> sensitize the relevant parts of government. It is the ethnic interest groups
> that remind U.S. officials of the moral considerations in our foreign
> policy.[1]

Whether a particular ethnic interest group can successfully impact American foreign

policy is dependent on several variables. The census data indicates that ethnic groups

exist with the requisite numbers to wield significant political power if properly motivated

to turnout for the vote. The two examples of the Jewish- and Irish-American

communities illustrate how this political power has been successfully translated into

foreign policy influence in the past. The experiences of Armenian- and Arab-Americans

illustrate the unsuccessful side of influence peddling while at the same time

demonstrating the capacity to learn from past mistakes.

In the current global environment, the opportunity exists for further ethnic group

influence, provided these groups can successfully convince policymakers their goals are

in keeping with today's broadly defined national interests. An appreciation of this

dynamic in the foreign policy formulation process is essential for those involved in both

the diplomatic and military professions. As the U.S. continues to espouse a policy of

engagement for virtually every corner of the earth, the picture of where national interests are clearly involved becomes increasingly blurred. Barring the reemergence of a peer competitor to focus our policy considerations or a demonstrated willingness on the part of our political leadership to apply a far more narrow interpretation of national interests, the current environment seems likely to continue.

Contrary to protestations from various circles that the often narrow, single-issue focus of these ethnic interest groups is somehow "un-American," as Mitchell Bard points out in this chapter's opening quotation, group concerns often serve as our moral compass in policy considerations. Far from being "un-American," taking advantage of the political process as it now exists is arguably the most American of activities.

As a consequence, the number of effective lobby groups will undoubtedly grow along with a corresponding increase in the number of voices seeking recognition within policy circles. At the same time the potential for a lack of coherency in U.S. foreign policy also increases, leaving allies and adversaries alike to guess at our intentions in a given situation. Given this increased potential for misunderstanding, the prudent military leader would be wise to recognize that literally any point on the globe could rapidly become a theater of operations. While the road from ethnic group interest to military involvement is long and winding, the record would seem to indicate that in our political system, where those who can deliver the votes hold enormous power, the decision to take the first steps down that path may be easier than anticipated.

Notes

[1] Mitchell Geoffrey Bard, *The Water's Edge and Beyond: Defining the Limits to Domestic Influence on United States Middle East Policy* (New Brunswick, N.J.: Transaction Publishers, 1991), 302.

Bibliography

Abbott, David W., and James P. Levine. *Wrong Winner: The Coming Debacle in the Electoral College.* New York: Praeger Publishers, 1991.

"Armenia." *Library of Congress Country Study*, n.p. On-line. Internet, 15 January 1999. Available from http://rs6.loc.gov/cgi-bin/query/r?frd/cstdy:@field(DOCID+am 0020.

Bard, Mitchell Geoffrey. *The Water's Edge and Beyond: Defining the Limits to Domestic Influence on United States Middle East Policy.* New Brunswick, New Jersey: Transaction Publishers, 1991.

Callahan, David. *Unwinnable Wars: American Power and Ethnic Conflict.* New York: Hill and Wang, 1997.

Chiswick, Barry R., and Teresa A. Sullivan. "The New Immigrants." In *State of the Union: America in the 1990s, Volume Two: Social Trends.* Edited by Reynolds Farley. New York: Russell Sage Foundation, 1995.

Clark, Dennis J. *Irish Blood: Northern Ireland and the American Conscience.* Port Washington, New York: Kennikat Press, 1977.

Coogan, Tim P. *The IRA: A History.* Niwot, Colorado: Roberts Rinehart Publishers, 1994.

Curtis, Richard H. *Stealth PACs: Lobbying Congress for Control of U.S. Middle East Policy.* Washington, D.C.: American Educational Trust, 1996.

Dawisha, Karen, and Bruce Parrott, eds. *Democratization and Authoritarianism in Postcommunist Societies.* Vol. 4, *Conflict, Cleavage, and Change in Central Asia and the Caucasus.* Cambridge, U.K.: Cambridge University Press, 1997.

Farley, Reynolds. *The New American Reality: Who We Are, How We Got Here, Where We Are Going.* New York: Russell Sage Foundation, 1996.

Gitlin, Todd. *The Twilight of Common Dreams: Why America is Wracked by Culture Wars.* New York: Metropolitan Books, 1995.

Glastris, Paul. "Multicultural Foreign Policy in Washington." In *U.S. News and World Report.* 21 July 1997, 32-35.

Glick, Edward B. *The Triangular Connection: America, Israel, and American Jews.* London: George Allen and Unwin (Publishers) Ltd., 1982.

Gunter, Michael M. *"Pursuing the Just Cause of Their People": A Study of Contemporary Armenian Terrorism.* New York: Greenwood Press, 1986.

Habermas, Jürgen. "On the Concept of Public Opinion." In *The Habermas Reader.* Edited by William Outhwaite. Oxford, U.K.: Blackwell Publishers Ltd, 1996.

Halley, Laurence. *Ancient Affections: Ethnic Groups and Foreign Policy.* New York: Praeger Publishers, 1985.

Hardin, Russell. *One for All: The Logic of Group Conflict.* Princeton, New Jersey: Princeton University Press, 1995.

Harrison, Roderick J., and Claudette E. Bennett. "Racial and Ethnic Diversity." In *State of the Union: America in the 1990s, Volume Two: Social Trends.* Edited by Reynolds Farley. New York: Russell Sage Foundation, 1995.

Hays, F. Wallace. "U.S. Congress and the Caspian." In *Caspian Crossroads* 3, no. 3 (Winter 1998): 8-11.

Holland, Jack. *The American Connection: U.S. Guns, Money, and Influence in Northern Ireland.* New York: Viking Press, 1987.

Howe, Russell W., and Sarah H. Trott. *The Power Peddlers: How Lobbyists Mold America's Foreign Policy.* Garden City, New York: Doubleday and Company, Inc., 1976.

Hudson, Michael C., and Ronald G. Wolfe, eds. *The American Media and the Arabs.* Washington, D.C.: Center for Contemporary Arab Studies, Georgetown University, 1980.

Huntington, Samuel P. *The Clash of Civilizations and the Remaking of World Order.* New York: Simon and Schuster, 1996.

Huntington, Samuel P., et al. *The Clash of Civilizations? The Debate: A Foreign Affairs Reader.* New York: Council on Foreign Relations, Inc., 1993.

Isaacs, Harold R. *Idols of the Tribe: Group Identity and Political Change.* New York: Harper and Row, Publishers, Inc., 1975.

Kelley, Kevin J. *The Longest War: Northern Ireland and the IRA.* Westport, Connecticut: Lawrence Hill and Company, Inc., 1988.

The Lausanne Treaty: Turkey and Armenia. New York: The American Committee Opposed to the Lausanne Treaty, 1926.

Levy, Mark R., and Michael S. Kramer. *The Ethnic Factor.* New York: Simon and Schuster, 1972.

Lilienthal, Alfred M. *The Zionist Connection: What Price Peace?* New York: Dodd, Mead and Company, 1978.

Missakian, J. *A Searchlight on the Armenian Question (1878-1950).* Boston: Hairenik Publishing Company, 1950.

Newland, Kathleen. "The Impact of U.S. Refugee Policies on U.S. Foreign Policy: A Case of the Tail Wagging the Dog?" In *Threatened Peoples, Threatened Borders: World Migration and U.S. Policy.* Edited by Michael S. Teitelbaum and Myron Weiner. New York: The American Assembly, 1995. 13, On-line. Internet, 15 January 1999. Available from http://www.ceip.org/people/migdog.htm.

News from Armenia and Artsakh/Karabagh, 4. On-line. Internet, 15 January 1999. Available from http://www.erols.com/guerig/v1/armenia.html.

Novak, Michael. *The Rise of the Unmeltable Ethnics: Politics and Culture in the Seventies.* New York: The Macmillan Company, 1972.

O'Ballance, Edgar. *Wars in the Caucasus, 1990-1995.* New York: New York University Press, 1997.

Papazian, Dennis R. "Armenians." *The Armenian Genocide* homepage, 11, On-line. Internet, 13 January 1999. Available from http://www.calpoly.edu/~pkiziria/pub-files/history.html.

Rubenberg, Cheryl A. *Israel and the American National Interest: A Critical Examination.* Urbana, Illinois: University of Illinois Press, 1986.

Said, Abdul Aziz, ed. *Ethnicity and U.S. Foreign Policy.* New York: Praeger Publishers, 1977.

Sheffer, Gabriel, ed. *Modern Diasporas in International Politics.* New York: St. Martin's Press, 1986.

Snow, Donald M., and Eugene Brown. *Beyond the Water's Edge: An Introduction to U.S. Foreign Policy.* New York: St. Martin's Press, 1997.

Spiegel, Steven L. "Ethnic Politics and the Formulation of U.S. Policy Toward the Arab-Israeli Dispute." In *Ethnic Groups and U.S. Foreign Policy.* Edited by Mohammed E. Ahari. New York: Greenwood Press, 1987.

Suny, Ronald Grigor, ed. *Transcaucasia, Nationalism, and Social Change: Essays in the History of Armenia, Azerbaijan, and Georgia.* Ann Arbor, Mich.: The University of Michigan Press, 1996.

Takaki, Ronald, ed. *From Different Shores: Perspectives on Race and Ethnicity in America.* 2nd ed. New York: Oxford University Press, 1994.

Trask, Roger R. *The United States Response to Turkish Nationalism and Reform, 1914-1939.* Minneapolis, Minn.: The University of Minnesota Press, 1971.

Trice, Robert H. "Domestic Interest Groups and the Arab-Israeli Conflict: A Behavioral Analysis." In *Ethnicity and U.S. Foreign Policy.* Edited by Abdul Aziz Said. New York: Praeger Publishers, 1977.

Watanabe, Paul Y. *Ethnic Groups, Congress, and American Foreign Policy: The Politics of the Turkish Arms Embargo.* Westport, Conn.: Greenwood Press, 1984.

Wilson, Woodrow, President. In Samuel P. Huntington, "The Erosion of American National Interests." In *Foreign Affairs,* 76, no. 5 (September/October 1997): 28-49.

Yankelovich, Daniel and I. M. Destler. *Beyond the Beltway: Engaging the Public in U.S. Foreign Policy.* New York: W. W. Norton and Company, 1994.